MW00579582

TABLE OF CONTENTS

DON MATTINGLY

Born: April 20, 1961, at Evansville, Indiana
Height: 6′0″
Weight: 175
High School: Evansville, Indiana; Memorial

In what could go down as one of the greatest bargains of all time, the New York Yankees were able to select first baseman Don Mattingly in the 19th round of the 1979 draft. Most teams passed on Mattingly because they expected him to attend college. When he decided to sign with the Yankees instead, the rest of the major league teams cringed.

But Mattingly did not become an instant sensation in the majors. There were four long years in the minor leagues, wondering if he would ever get the chance at the major league level. His prowess at the plate was already beginning to show, as witnessed by his averaging better than .300 all four years. Finally, he got his chance in 1983, but played in just 91 games, hitting .283.

The 1984 season was when the real Don Mattingly began to show itself. He led the American League with a .343 average (batting 603 times) and he also led the league in hits with 207 and doubles with 44. He continued his startling consistency in 1985 and produced his best numbers in '86.

Mattingly batted 677 times, hit .352, led the league with 238 hits and also paced the league in doubles for the third consecutive season with 53. Other categories he led the league in were slugging percentage (.573), total bases (388) and extra-base hits (86).

More notably, Mattingly has put numbers in the books that bring back memories of former Yankee greats. Those 388 total bases were the most by a Yankee since Joe DiMaggio's 418 in 1937. He was the first Yankee to hit .350 or better since Mickey Mantle in 1957 and his 53 doubles broke the team record set by Lou Gehrig in 1927. To top it off, he is the first Yankee to lead the team in average, hits, doubles and runs batted in for three straight years since Gehrig did it from 1932-34.

Mattingly has driven in at least 110 runs three consecutive seasons and entered the 1986 campaign having played in 282 straight games. It's no wonder he is re-writing the book on hitting.

Batting Statistics

	AB	H	2B	3B	HR	RBI	Avg.
Career-5 Years	2223	737	160	11	93	401	.332

ROGER CLEMENS

Born: August 4, 1962, at Dayton, Ohio
Height: 6′4″
Weight: 215
College: University of Texas
High School: Houston, Texas; Spring Woods

Boston Red Sox pitcher Roger Clemens is a relative newcomer on the major league scene. But his performance in 1986, as the Red Sox advanced to the World Series against the New York Mets, was one for the ages. It was one of those years where everything just went right.

Clemens started the year by winning his first 14 games, the fifth-best start in major league history. During that streak, Clemens established a major league record by striking out 20 Seattle Mariners in an April 29 game. His control was so exemplary, Clemens allowed no walks in that game.

Perhaps his biggest thrill was starting the All-Star Game for the American League and pitching three scoreless innings. In that stint, Clemens threw 25 pitches, of which 21 were strikes.

He finished the '86 season with a league-high 24 wins against only four losses and his 2.48 earned run average was also best in the league. He also struck out 238 batters in 254 innings.

Ironically, Clemens almost pitched for the Mets, the team he faced in the '86 World Series. He was selected by the Mets in the 12th round of the 1981 amateur draft after high school. But because of that relatively late selection, he opted to attend college at the University of Texas where he compiled a 25-7 record in two seasons, striking out 241 batters in 275 innings.

In the 1983 draft, Clemens was chosen in the first round by the Red Sox and decided to leave college. He pitched a total of just 128 innings in the minor leagues in 1983 and '84 before being promoted to the Red Sox during the '84 season.

The awards came fast and furious after 1986. He became the first pitcher to win the league Most Valuable Player award, Cy Young award and be named Most Valuable Player in the All-Star Game in the same season. He was voted unanimously as the Cy Young award winner and the MVP honor can be traced to one telling statistic: Clemens won 14 games following a Red Sox defeat.

Pitching Statistics

	Won	Lost	SO	BB	ERA
Career—3 Years	40	13	438	133	3.15

WADE BOGGS

Born: June 15, 1958, at Omaha, Nebraska
Height: 6′2″
Weight: 197
College: Hillsborough Community College
High School: Tampa, Florida; H.B. Plant

Boston Red Sox third baseman Wade Boggs was only 18 years old when he was selected in the seventh round of the 1976 draft. A standout in high school, Boggs figured to make a quick run through the minors before advancing to the major leagues. But it took longer than expected.

His first season of organized baseball was spent at Elmira in the New York-Pennsylvania League and he hit just .263. It was hard to imagine Boggs becoming one of the game's best hitters.

His ability began showing the following year at Winston-Salem of the Carolina League where he hit .332. Not since that season has Boggs' average been below .300 at the end of a season.

Still, promotion to the majors was coming slowly. In fact, Boggs spent six seasons in the minors until finally making the Red Sox roster in 1982. He hasn't looked back since.

In five major league seasons from 1982-86, Boggs has led the American League in hitting three times and his lowest average was .325 in 1984. While he led the league in hitting with a .357 average in 1986, and the Red Sox advanced to the World Series, it was still a traumatic year for the family-oriented man.

He was hitting .380 after flirting with the .400 mark in early June when his mother was killed in a June 17 car accident. His concentration shattered, Boggs hit .247 during the month of July, the worst hitting month of his career. He gradually regained his composure and hit .353 in August and an astounding .398 in September.

A student of hitting, Boggs also walked 105 times in 1986, becoming the first player in history to have 200 hits and 100 walks in the same season. His .453 on-base percentage led the majors as did his 312 times on base by hit, walk or hit batsman.

Although Boggs doesn't drive in large totals of runs, he is still a clutch hitter. In 1986, he hit .359 with runners in scoring position and succeeded 17 of 24 times (.708) in getting a runner home from third with less than two outs.

Batting Statistics

	AB	H	2B	3B	HR	RBI	Avg.
Career—5 Years	2778	978	178	17	32	322	.352

FERNANDO VALENZUELA

Born: November 1, 1960, at Navajoa, Sonora, Mexico
Height: 5'11"
Weight: 180

He has quietly become one of major league baseball's most consistent pitchers. And Fernando Valenzuela of the Los Angeles Dodgers owes much of his success to a journeyman pitcher in the Dodgers' organization. The time was the fall of 1979. Valenzuela had begun his pitching career as an 18-year-old, playing for Guanajuato in the Mexican Central League. The following year he was pitching for Yucatan in the Mexican League when the Dodgers began to notice. His contract was purchased by Los Angeles on July 6, 1979, and he pitched three games for the Dodgers' Lodi affiliate in the California League that summer.

It was the post-season that would start Valenzuela on the road to stardom. At the Arizona Instructional League, he learned how to throw the screwball from pitcher Bobby Castillo. National League hitters have regretted that development ever since.

Valenzuela became a fulltime major league pitcher during the strike-shortened 1981 season and he took the league by storm. He led the league with 180 strikeouts in just 192 innings.

From 1984-86, Valenzuela struck out more than 200 batters each season and his best pitching probably came during the '86 campaign. On a Dodgers team that had one of its worst seasons in years, Valenzuela was the glue that held the club together. His 21 victories (against just 11 losses) led the National League as did his 20 complete games.

Because of that darting screwball, Valenzuela is especially difficult to hit against at night. In 1986, he was 16-6 in night games and only 5-5 in daylight. His 84 victories is the most for a National League pitcher during the last five seasons.

In the off-season, Valenzuela is active with youth, coordinating a "Be Smart, Stay in School" program that rewards those with perfect school attendance.

Pitching Statistics

	Won	Lost	SO	BB	ERA
Career—7 Years	99	68	1274	540	2.94

EDDIE MURRAY

Born: February 24, 1956, at Los Angeles, California
Height: 6'2"
Weight: 215
High School: Los Angeles, Calif.; Locke

When one thinks of consistency in major league baseball, the name of Baltimore Orioles first baseman Eddie Murray immediately comes to mind. A close look at the numbers he has compiled in 10 years with the Orioles is testimony to that. One thing is clear: you can count on Eddie Murray.

Not including 1981, a season shortened by a players' strike, or 1986, when he landed on the disabled list for the first time in his career, here are some of the eerie consistencies put together by the sweet-swinging lefty:

From 1980-85, there were runs batted in totals of 116, 110, 111, 110 and 124; batting averages of .300, .316, .306 twice and .297 and home run totals of 32, 32, 33, 29 and 31. From 1977-85, his hit totals read like a broken record: 173, 174, 179, 186, 174, 178, 180 and 183.

His totals for doubles in that period fluctuated between 26 and 37 and his games played (aside from 1981 and '86) have never dipped below 151.

But 1986 was a season of frustration. The Orioles had one of their worst seasons in memory and Murray missed 25 games with injuries. Still, he led the team in hitting at .305 and with 84 RBIs. It was the seventh consecutive season he led the team in that category.

Entering the 1987 season, Murray ranked second among major league players in game-winning RBIs, a tribute to his ability as a clutch hitter. His 101 game-winners was second only to Keith Hernandez of the New York Mets, who had 107. And Hernandez built his lead with 13 such RBIs in 1986 to Murray's four.

A dedicated athlete on and off the field, Murray heads the "Carrie Murray Outdoor Educational Campus," a contribution to the city of Baltimore which seeks to provide to every school child in Baltimore the opportunity to participate in the camp. The program is in honor of his mother.

Batting Statistics

	AB	H	2B	3B	HR	RBI	Avg.
Career—10 Years	5624	1679	296	20	275	1015	.299

GEORGE BRETT

Born: May 15, 1953, at Glendale, West Virginia
Height: 6′0″
Weight: 195
High School: El Segundo, California

Perhaps one of the best pure hitters in major league baseball, Kansas City Royals third baseman just has to find a way to be able to stay on the field. An assortment of injuries have conspired to limit his playing time—and effectiveness—in the last few seasons.

Actually, the 1985 season was one Brett will always remember. He stayed healthy, playing in 155 games (compared to 104 the year before) and batted .335. He also hit a career-high 30 home runs and drove in 112 runs, pacing the Royals to the championship of the American League Western Division. The Royals then went on to beat the St. Louis Cardinals in the World Series.

But in 1986, there were more injuries and he played in just 124 games. While leading the club with a .290 batting average, it was only the fourth time in his career that his batting average dipped below .300 for a season. He still managed to hit 16 home runs and drive in 73 runs.

However, when all is said and done, Brett will probably remember 1980 as his most exciting season ever. Despite missing 45 games, Brett flirted with the .400 mark thanks to an incredible hitting streak after the All-Star Game; a game he missed because of an injury.

When regular play resumed, Brett hit safely in 63 of 72 games, batting .420 with 54 runs, 16 homers and 77 RBI. He first went over .400 on August 17 and the latest he was at .400 was on September 19. He couldn't maintain the frantic pace and ended the season with a .390 average, the highest in the major leagues since Ted Williams hit .406 in 1941.

His 118 RBI in 117 games made him the 17th player in history to drive in at least 100 runs and average at least one RBI a game.

Even though 1986 was a season to forget for several reasons, Brett still reached some milestones. He was voted to his 11th straight All-Star Game and came up with his 2,000th hit, his 200th home run and his 1,000 RBI. He was only the seventh active player to attain those milestones.

Batting Statistics

	AB	H	2B	3B	HR	RBI	Avg.
Career—14 Years	6675	2095	428	112	209	1050	.314

DALE MURPHY

Born: March 12, 1956, at Portland, Oregon
Height: 6′4″
Weight: 215
College: Brigham Young University
High School: Portland, Oregon; Woodrow Wilson

Day after day, he simply goes out to center field and does his job. It's almost possible to take Dale Murphy of the Atlanta Braves for granted. But his accomplishments don't allow that.

Certainly, durability and dependability are high atop the list of attributes used to describe Murphy. Of course, you can't overlook the hitting, either.

Murphy has spent just one, two-month stint on the disabled list during his 11-year career, and that was back in 1979. In four of the last five years, he played in all 162 games. In fact, he had a four-year streak at that figure until playing in "only" 160 games in 1986.

When he sat out for a game on July 9, 1986, in Philadelphia, it snapped a streak of 740 consecutive games dating back to September 27, 1981. That 740-game streak ranks as the 11th-highest in major league history.

But when you talk about Dale Murphy, hitting usually takes the front seat. He has hit 33 or more home runs in a season five times and his 1986 total of 29 was the first sub-30 season after four straight with 30 or more round trippers. Those four seasons were models of consistency, as Murphy hit 36 three years in a row and then 37 in 1985.

His 174 home runs since 1982 are second only to Mike Schmidt's total of 181 and his 524 RBI in that same period trails only Eddie Murray (539), Dave Winfield (540) and Jim Rice (558).

The statistics Murphy has compiled during his career are second only in Atlanta history to Hall of Famer Hank Aaron. Murphy was voted to the National League All-Star team in 1986 for the fifth straight time and he has also made the All-Star team in six of the last seven years.

Murphy also writes a weekly column every Sunday for the Atlanta Journal/Constitution. However, instead of being paid, he and the newspaper offer a four-year college scholarship to a high school graduate each year.

Batting Statistics

	AB	H	2B	3B	HR	RBI	Avg.
Career—11 Years	5017	1388	214	32	266	822	.277

OZZIE SMITH

Born: December 26, 1954, at Mobile, Alabama
Height: 5'10"
Weight: 155
College: California Polytechnic State University at
San Luis Obispo

The Wizard. The Wizard of Oz. Take your pick. Those are the words used to describe St. Louis Cardinals shortstop Ozzie Smith. Some have said he may be the best fielding shortstop in history.

That might be forgetting some great defensive players who didn't have the benefit of artificial turf, but watch Smith over the course of a season and you're left shaking your head in amazement time after time.

Modest and unassuming, Smith is a tireless worker who has also become a solid hitter. He batted a career-high .280 in 1986 with 54 RBI. But it's his glove that receives the rave reviews.

Once asked about being the best ever, Smith said, "That's kind of scary when you hear that, but I don't get caught up in it. There's a lot of good shortstops around. As a major leaguer, you should be able to do the fundamentals. You should make the good plays."

Smith goes one step better than that: he makes the spectacular plays seem almost commonplace. When he was acquired from San Diego in February, 1982, St. Louis players figured Smith was the missing link, that he could help the team win the pennant. The Cardinals won the World Series that season and since Smith's arrival have been in two fall classics.

Los Angeles Times columnist Jim Murray once described Smith by writing, "He has made the ground single to the outfield in left extinct. The turf between second and third on any diamond he plays becomes the Land of Oz. Other guys play shortstop. Ozzie plays over the rainbow. It's his yellow brick road."

"He's airborne so much of the time he could probably cross the Mississippi without getting his feet wet. Bojangles in cleats."

The numbers? He has led National League shortstops in fielding percentage five times and in assists five times. He has won seven consecutive Gold Gloves for fielding prowess.

The Wizard of Oz. There's no place like short.

Batting Statistics

	AB	H	2B	3B	HR	RBI	Avg.
Career—9 Years	4739	1169	179	38	13	374	.247

MIKE SCOTT

Born: April 26, 1955, at Santa Monica, Florida
Height: 6′3″
Weight: 215
College: Pepperdine University
High School: Hawthorne, California

Spread those fingers wide. Wider. Put a baseball in there. Throw it. Control it. Watch it dip and dance. Watch batters pound their bats in frustration. Listen to managers complain that the ball is scuffed. Watch Mike Scott smile.

Mike Scott of the Houston Astros has been smiling for two years now, ever since learning how to throw a split-fingered fastball after the 1984 season. Ironically, he was taught the pitch by Roger Craig, then out of baseball. Craig is now the manager of division-rival San Francisco and a frequent complainer that Scott is defacing the baseball, making it do tricks.

Said Scott, reflecting on the '84 season in which he was 5-11 with an earned run average of 4.68, "I was worried I might have to start looking for work in California or Arizona." Instead, he went to Craig.

"After I threw that pitch for a day or two, I knew I was going to be using it quite a bit." Indeed, he has.

The '85 season started slowly as Scott learned the best time to throw the pitch and how to control it. On June 26 he was 5-4 but went 13-4 the rest of the way. In '86, Scott was 18-8 with a league-high 306 strikeouts and 2.22 ERA. His record would have been better with more run production from the Houston offense.

He captured the National League Cy Young award, but his most breathtaking accomplishment came September 25, when he pitched a no-hitter as the Astros clinched their division. In '86, he struck out at least nine batters in a game 19 times and hurled five shutouts.

Thank you, Roger.

Said Scott, "When you stop and think about it, it's amazing what a difference that one pitch has made. I don't know where I'd be without it."

Pitching Statistics

	Won	Lost	SO	BB	ERA
Career—8 Years	65	62	750	363	3.70

MIKE SCHMIDT

Born: September 27, 1949, at Dayton, Ohio
Height: 6′2″
Weight: 203
College: Ohio University
Degree: Bachelor of Arts in Business Administration
High School: Dayton, Ohio; Fairview

Like a fine wine that ages and seems to get better with time, Mike Schmidt of the Philadelphia Phillies just watches his value soar. It seems like an eternity since 1973, when he became a fulltime player for the Phillies and batted just .196 in 132 games.

But the seeds of growth were there in his 18 home runs that season. It became the start of a legend in Philadelphia that culminated with his 500th career home run early in the 1987 season.

Said Reggie Jackson, who ranked sixth on the all-time list with 548 homers before the start of the '87 season. "I'm a statistics nut and I figure if you hit 20 homers a year for 20 years, you still fall 100 short of 500. If you hit 30 a year for 15 years, you're still 50 short. When you think about it, it's pretty amazing."

Since that '73 season, Schmidt has led or tied for the league lead in homers eight times, has led or tied in RBI on four occasions and won the National League Most Valuable Player award three times. Only Schmidt, Stan Musial and Roy Campanella won the league MVP three times.

Schmidt's third came in 1986 at the age of 36, although he turned 37 in September. He tied a career high playing in 160 games, batted .290 and led the league in home runs with 37 and in RBI with 119.

Schmidt moved back to third base in '86 after playing first base for a large part of the 1985 season. He was so happy with the return to familiar surroundings that Schmidt made just eight errors during the season (six at third base), a career low. He captured his 10th Gold Glove for fielding excellence.

It seems Schmidt keeps getting better and a changed attitude has helped. Since changing his batting style on August 15, 1985, Schmidt batted .298 with 51 homers and 155 RBI in 208 games. And he plays every game as if it could be his last.

Asked about Hall of Fame consideration down the road, he said, "I hardly ever think about things like that. Sometimes I play like it's the first game of my career. I get butterflies before the game and sometimes during the game."

Most would say it's the pitchers getting the butterflies when Mike Schmidt is in the game.

Batting Statistics

	AB	H	2B	3B	HR	RBI	Avg.
Career—15 Years	7292	1954	352	57	495	1392	.268

RYNE SANDBERG

Born: September 18, 1959, at Spokane, Washington
Height: 6′2″
Weight: 180
High School: Spokane, Washington; North Central

He had bounced around the Philadelphia Phillies' organization for four years wondering when he would get the chance. He even started out as a shortstop. But that all ended on January 27, 1982, when Ryne Sandberg was traded with shortstop Larry Bowa by the Phillies to the Chicago Cubs for shortstop Ivan DeJesus.

In a way, Sandberg can thank his lucky stars that Dallas Green was hired as the Cubs' general manager. Green had been in the Philadelphia organization and was familiar with the Phillies' young players.

Said Green, after making the deal, "If there had been no Ryne, there would have been no deal."

Chicago put Sandberg right on the field and let him play. He spent most of his time at third base in '82 but became the Cubs' fulltime second baseman the following year. He showed flashes in '82 and '83, batting .271 and .261, and combining for 15 home runs and 102 RBI.

It turned out 1984 was the year to remember. Sandberg paced the Cubs to the National League East title, and was named Major League Player of the Year by The Sporting News. He hit .314, led the league in runs scored with 114 and in triples with 19. He added 200 hits, 19 home runs and 84 RBI.

The next two seasons saw the Cubs' fortunes change, but Sandberg continued to display his talent, although the numbers were also off from that glorious 1984.

Still, many players would settle for years of .305 and .284 in 1985 and '86, along with 26 home runs and 83 RBI in '85 and 14 homers and 76 RBI in '86.

Out of the batter's box, Sandberg has also become a proficient fielder. He led National League second basemen in assists in 1984 and '86 and has had the best fielding percentage among league second basemen in three of the last four seasons. He made just five errors in 801 chances in 1986.

Perhaps Sandberg's ability is best summed up by former player John Vukovich, a coach with the Cubs: "I wouldn't want Ryno's money or his fame or his youth or his looks," Vukovich said. "I'd like just to be able to play baseball the way he does for one day—one day—just to see what it feels like to be that good and make it look that easy."

Batting Statistics

	AB	H	2B	3B	HR	RBI	Avg.
Career—6 Years	3146	902	153	39	74	345	.287